B-25
MITCHELL
in action

by Ernest R. McDowell

illustrated by Don Greer

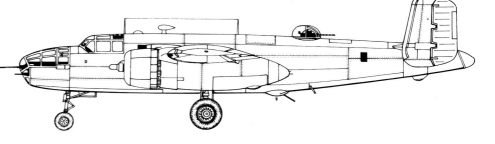

 squadron/signal publications

A B-25J of the 445 BS, 321 BG, 12th Air Force dodges an Fw 190 on its return to Corsica after a mission over Southern France in support of Operation "Anvil". This particular aircarft returned to the U.S. at the end of war, a veteran of 137 missions.

If you have any photographs of the aircraft, armor, soldiers or ships of any nation, particularly wartime snapshots, why not share them with us and help make Squadron/Signal's books all the more interesting and complete in the future. Any photograph sent to us will be copied and the original returned. The donor will be fully credited for any photos used. Please indicate if you wish us not to return the photos. Please send them to: Squadron/Signal Publications, Inc., 1115 Crowley Dr., Carrollton, TX 75011-5010.

TO: Robert C. Jones, Thomas McCann and Joseph Brilando.

A Special Acknowledgement of Appreciation for their help to:

Norman L. Avery, Fred C. Dickey, Malcom Long, David Lucabaugh, MSGT David Menard, Dana Bell and Capt. Peter R. Hefler.

Photo Credits

USAF Museum
USAF AAVS (MAC)
IPMS-USA
Capt. J.J. McKinstry Chapter
Norman L. Avery
William J. Balogh, Jr.
William Bennett
Fred C. Dickey, Jr.
Garry L. Fry

Richard M. Hill
Robert C. Jones
Michel Lavigne
Malcolm Long
David Lucabaugh
MSGT David W. Menard USAF
Eric Nicolle
John Preston

Juraj Rajinec
Felix Rameder
Earl Reinert
Dr. Robert Rose
Kenn C. Rust
Pat Stein
David Weatherill
Phil Yant

Lt. Col. James Doolittle taking off from the deck of USS Hornet enroute to Tokyo. (USAF)

North American B-25 Mitchell

In 1938 the United States Army Air Force issued a circular proposal, Specification Number 98-102, which called for a twin-engined medium attack bomber. North American Aviation, Inc. of Inglewood, California, in an attempt to meet these requirements and win a contract, initiated a design proposal which they designated NA–40-1. This design called for a twin-engined, twin-tailed, tricycle landing geared, high wing monoplane of a rather clean aerodynamic configuration. The pilot and co-pilot were to be seated in tandem in a long greenhouse type cockpit similar to that of the Martin B-10 bomber and North American's own 0-47. The bombardier-navigator was to be housed in a glazed nose that afforded excellent forward and down vision. As an attack bomber the NA-40-1 provided the bombardier with a single .30 Cal. M-2 machine gun mounted in a rotating nose blister. Two fixed forward firing .30s were to be mounted in each wing. A dorsal turret of the powered type was to be operated by a radio-gunner and the fifth crewman would handle two more .30s, one mounted to fire downward through the floor and the other to be located in a mid upper position. Each gun was to carry 500 rounds of ammunition. The maximum bomb load would be 1,200 pounds and 476 gallons of fuel would feed the two Pratt & Whitney R-1830-s6C3-G Twin Wasp radial engines that developed 1,100 horsepower each. This all added up to a gross weight of 19,500 pounds. As the design looked very good, work soon commenced on a prototype aircraft.

In January 1939 the prototype was rolled out and test flown by N.A. test pilot Paul Balfour. The top speed turned out to be a disappointing 265 miles per hour but the design obviously held a great deal of promise so the design team set to work to improve the performance figures.

To increase speed the Pratt and Whitney engines were replaced by Wright Cyclones producing 1,350 hp for take off, also radial engines. The aircraft, now redesignated the NA-40-2 or NA-40B was flown from Los Angeles to Wright Field at Dayton, Ohio in March for official Air Corps evaluation. Maximum speed now was 285 mph even though gross weight had increased to 21,000 pounds. The Air Corps put the plane through two weeks of testing and was impressed with the results. Turning the NA-40B over to the attack bomber test program for further evaluation resulted in the destruction of the prototype. Major Younger Pitts took it up and ran through some tests. However, while attempting to turn into Wright Field approach he lost control and crashed at a high rate of speed.

The company had planned export versions of the original design up to a proposed NA-40-7 design, but the Air Corps asked for a number of modifications and changes. North American management asked R.H. Rice and J.L. Atwood to redesign the airplane. The new prototype was given the company designation NA-62. When finished, it had the appearance which was to remain pretty much constant throughout the entire series. To accomodate the doubled bomb load the Air Corps demanded, the greenhouse for pilot and co-pilot was eliminated by raising the fuselage. The wing attachment point was lowered from a shoulder location to midwing which gave a better main spar location within the fuselage. This change improved aerodynamic design as well as altering the general aspect of the airplane. The engine nacelles were cleaned up in profile and extended aft of the wing. A tail cone with hand held .50 caliber machine gun increased firepower. The bombardier's compartment was modified to blend into the new fuselage, thus eliminating the bulbous nose. The Army approved the NA-62 on 10 September 1939. The outbreak of war in Europe caused the Air Corps to forego further prototyping. The need for aircraft production was so urgent that for all practical purposes the NA-40B served as the XB-25.

NA-40 in the final stage of construction. This first prototype was powered by P&W R-1830 engines which gave the plane disappointing performance. Note the extensive nose glazing is covered during construction. [N.L. Avery]

Development

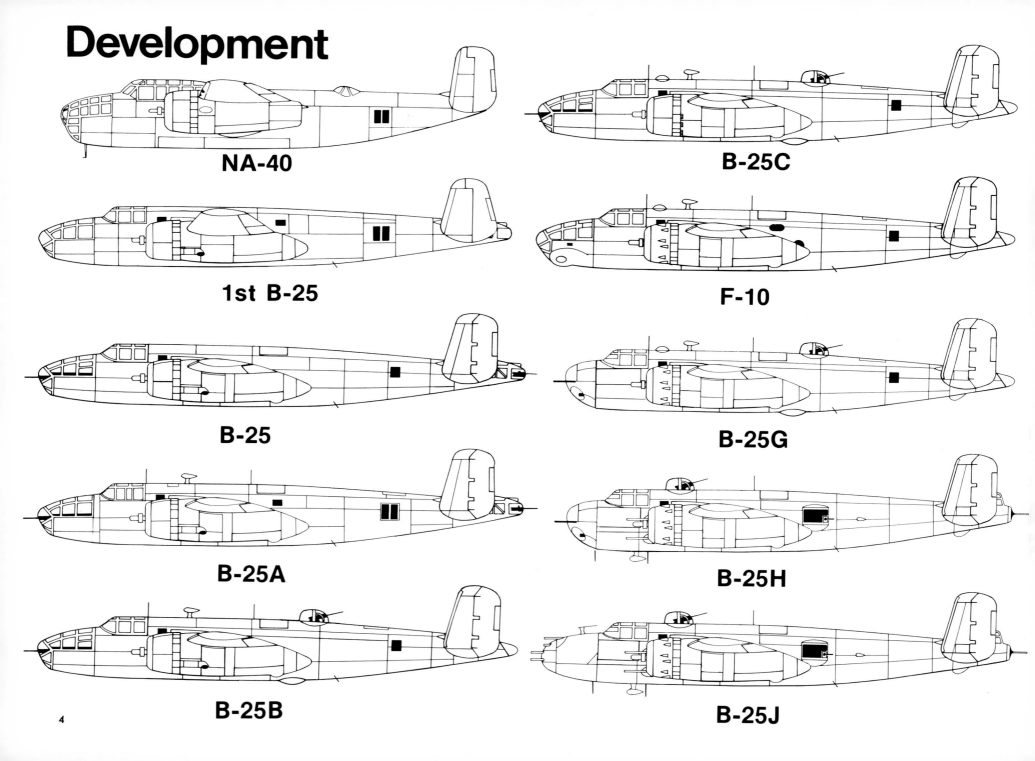

NA-40

1st B-25

B-25

B-25A

B-25B

B-25C

F-10

B-25G

B-25H

B-25J

NA-40B, with the high degree of shine all demonstration models sported, on the line at Wright Field, Dayton, Ohio, 22 March 1939. Wright Cyclones have replaced the inadequate Pratt & Whitney engines. [USAF via D.W. Lucabaugh]

Nose Variations

NA-40

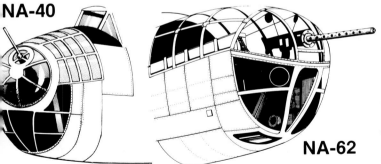

NA-62

[Above Right & Right] B-25 Number One, known as NA-62 by the manufacturer, shows the radical redesign that has taken place. The fuselage is now much shallower, the "greenhouse" replaced by a more conventional stepped canopy. The twin tails also have a new shape, which proved unsatisfactory and was soon changed to the final configuration. The plane [40-2165] is seen as it appeared at Mines Field in August 1940. [F.C. Dickey]

B-25(NA-62)

On 20 September 1939 a production contract valued at $11,771,000 was awarded to North American for 184 aircraft to be designated as the B-25. North American had assigned the manufacturer's number NA-62 to the design. An airframe was delivered on 4 July to Wright Field, Ohio for static testing. The initial airplane bore a family resemblance to the NA-40 with its shining bare metal finish and an unbroken wing dihedral. A total of 195,000 + engineering manhours plus 8,500 new engineering drawings were expended on the NA-62. The first fully completed B-25 made its initial test flight on 19 August 1940.

Sent to the USAAF testing grounds at Wright Field and run through a series of test flights, the aircraft seemed to have only marginal directional stability. The fault seemed to be caused by excessive dihedral. This was rectified by altering the outer wing panels to an absolute horizontal position. This gave the B-25 its characteristic gull winged look, which remained unchanged through the production life of the series. The new wing geometry was installed on the 10th production aircraft. A total of twenty four B-25s were delivered during 1940 before the model gave way to the B model. About this time the name "Mitchell" was given to the B-25, honoring the late General Billy Mitchell whom many consider the father of modern American military aviation.

The B-25 featured a five man crew. The pilot and co-pilot were seated side by side in the redesigned fuselage. The tail gunner operated a single .50 caliber machine gun in a glazed stinger in the tail from a prone position. A .30 caliber machine gun with a rather limited field of fire was mounted in a socket in the nose to be manned by the bombardier. Other .30 machine guns were located in the sides of the fuselage and in the roof of the fuselage aft of the wing. The fuselage was of semi-monocoque aluminum alloy construction with alclad alloy skin. The portion of the fuselage above the wing and between the front spar and trailing edge was permanently attached to the wing and was removable with the center section. The wings were the cantilever type with a mid-level position. All metal construction was used on the wings which were divided into five sections, including the center section that could be detached from the remainder of the fuselage, outer wing sections detachable from the center section and removable wing tips. The outer wing sections were the single spar type with alclad skinning, ailerons were metal with fabric covering. The B-25 had hydraulically operated slotted wing flaps in two sections. The tail section was a cantilever monoplane type, all metal with twin fins and rudders. The tricycle landing gear was fully retractable and hydraulically operated. Three bladed Hamilton Standard constant-speed, full-feathering propellors with anti-icers and twin Wright Cyclone GR-2600-A5B engines produced 1,350 horse power at 2300 rpm at 5,000 feet, with a maximum take-off rating of 1,600 horse power at 2400 rpm. Internal bomb storage was provided in the fuselage beneath the center section for a ton and a half of bombs. The B-25's top speed was 332 mph.

The first operational group to fly the new bomber was the 17th Bombardment Group (Medium) which began to receive their B-25s in 1941. The 17th was based at McChord Field, Washington and began to fly coastal patrols after the attack on Pearl Harbor. They continued this activity after being transferred to Pendleton, Oregon. Moving east to the Lexington County Air Port in South Carolina they carried on patrols over the Atlantic Ocean before

another station change took them to Barksdale Air Field in Louisiana and more patrol duties over the Gulf of Mexico. The 17th thus became the first unit to act as coastal defenders over the waters of the entire coastal area of the United States. The B-25 is credited with being the first American bomber to sink an Axis submarine in the Atlantic Ocean in American territorial waters. It had already been given credit for getting a Japanese sub in the Pacific.

This B-25 was one of the original service test aircraft that was assigned to the 17th Bombardment Group's 95th Bomb Squadron and is one of the straight wing B-25s from the initial production batch. The Group was on maneuvers at the time this photo was taken at Felts Field in Washington. The obvious difference from the No. 1 craft is the "production" tail. [Lin Hendrix]

Another of the first nine B-25s produced with the straight wing. This also was a 95th Bomb Squadron aircraft. The Squadron was the first to sink an Axis submarine, getting it on 24 December 1941. The sinking was accomplished by Bombardier George Hammond who was in Brick Holstrom's crew. Because the crew had forgotten to take off the pitot tube cover, Hammond had to use his foot as a bomb sight. Nevertheless he laid one right on the conning tower of the Japanese craft. Holstrom later was one of the Doolittle raiders. [Lin Hendrix]

A close up of the same aircraft shows the insignia of 95 BS and aircraft number 11. Many of the 17th's crew became members of the Doolittle Group after flying the B-25s at Felts and later at Columbia, SC. [Lin Hendrix]

The inspection of the 95th Squadron by General Currie at Felts Field, Washington in July 1941. Capt. E.J. York, in the foreground, was later promoted to Major and at the time was the Squadron CO. He later became one of the Doolittle Raiders and was the one who landed in Russia, being the only one who spoke Russian. Some Russian pilots had been sent to Felts to learn the B-25 which they flew like pursuit ships. The 55th Pursuit, equipped with P-43s, was in Oregon at the time and used to like to dogfight with the Russians. This resulted in rivets popping from the wings of B-25s and tail gunners with cracked ribs. One P-43 pilot was actually forced into the ground near Eugene, Oregon. [Lin Hendrix]

B-25A

When theory is put into action, it is often found wanting. Such was the case at the start of World War II with bombers and the role in which they were to be employed. By definition every bomber had to operate over enemy-held territory during its mission. In carrying out its role, it becomes exposed to any actions the enemy can take to reduce its effectiveness, including fighter interceptions and anti-aircraft weapons fire from the ground. Quite early in European action it became painfully evident that lightly armed bombers were no match for enemy fighters. Even escorted bombers could not be protected 100 % by their own fighters in the face of determined attacks. Also escorting fighters were powerless to protect the bombers against flak. As these truths were brought home in early battles, the planners had to do something to counteract these hazards as much as possible. This meant increasing the defensive firepower of the individual bomber and doing whatever might be possible to provide added protection for the aircraft and its crew from flak. The latter could be implemented much faster than the former.

In the case of the North American Mitchell, this action resulted in the first model change and produced the B-25A. Self-sealing fuel tanks were installed to cut down the danger of fire and the pilots were given some armor plates as personal protection. Hopefully these changes would be useful against aircraft and flak both. These modifications commenced with the 25th model on the assembly line. The air crews always welcomed anything that added to the survivial rate.

However, to make these modifications it was necessary to sacrifice something in return. Maximum fuel capacity was reduced by 246 gallons and the range fell off 750 miles. The maximum gross weight increased 210 pounds while top speed dropped from 322 mph to 315 mph. Service ceiling was down from 30,000 feet to 27,000 feet and the rate of climb suffered slightly. The B-25A was eleven inches higher than the B-25, otherwise the aircraft were for the most part identical. Forty B-25As were produced.

The mark of a good basic design is it can be changed to suit new conditions with a minimum of difficulty and not suffer unduly in the process. The B-25 design was to prove over and over the soundness of the original aircraft design as it underwent many changes during the course of the war and even after the end of the war and remained a first line aircraft throughout its service life.

B-25As on the flight ramp at North American Inglewood early in the war. [N. Avery]

This B-25A of 17 Bomb Group is believed to be the Group COs aircraft. The Group insignia is on the nose. The aircraft number, one, is on the fin and is repeated on the nose. 17B indicates the Group number. [D.W. Lucabaugh]

A B-25A-NA [40-2189] pictured on a flight from its base at Wright Field, Ohio on 9 October 1944. Note the last two digits of the serial chalked on its nose. [D.W. Lucabaugh]

The 310 Bomb Group marking is shown on the Fin and rudder of this B-25A named "Millie" it is a Yellow band outlined in Blue. This shot was taken in North Africa. [P. Stein]

A B-25B in markings of Col. Doolittle. After the Tokyo Raid, the USAF painted up a number of Bs in Doolittle markings for publicity purposes. As with all other planes on the raid, Doolittle's plane was lost. [F.C. Dickey]

B-25B (Mitchell I)

While the A model was an attempted solution to the problem of providing additional crew protection, it remained for the B to resolve the problem of increased defensive firepower. North America began by removing all machine guns except the one mounted in the bombardier's nose compartment. The tail cone was reduced considerably in size, shortening the fuselage one foot two inches. A glazed area was kept to serve as a prone observation post. A photographic station was added just forward of this position. Bendix electrically operated turrets were incorporated into the fuselage in dorsal and ventral locations with twin .50 caliber machine guns in each. The ventral turret was fully retractable and was operated by a gunner who kneeled over a periscope-gunsight, a most uncomfortable position if the position had to be manned for any length of time.

The British had been experimenting with powered turrets for some time before the war as it had become increasingly clear that as speed increased the exposed gunner's position became more difficult to man. Turrets seemed to be the answer as they offered protection for the gunner, made for better accuracy, and were better gunnery platforms. It was also possible to operated multiple guns and obtain a devastating cone of fire. Ideally the aircraft should be designed around its turrets as they were extremely complex and bulky gadgets. Space had to be provided for the gunner and his equipment and in turn he had to ride the guns and turn as they turned to give smooth tracking of the target. The turrets that operated in a 360 degree arc had to obtain electrical power during rotation. A fire interrupter system had to be provided to prevent the gunner from shooting bits and pieces off his own aircraft while tracking an enemy plane. It had to be mounted so as to produce as little drag on the aircraft as possible. Mounting had to be accomplished without sacrificing the structural integrity of the fuselage. Its effect on the center of gravity had to be calculated and then compensated for by the design team. Personal equipment for the aerial gunner such as parachute, oxygen flasks, intercom, electrical heating outlet for his flying suit, life preserver, and other items as the mission or theatre required, had to be fitted either into or onto the turret.

That North American's people were able to incorporate not one but two turrets, one of which retracted, into the B-25B and still produce 100 of the aircraft during 1941 is an engineering marvel. How well they did the job is reflected in performance and specification figures. The B models maximum weight was upped to 28,460 pounds, an increase of just 1,360 pounds over the A. Top speed decreased a mere 15 mph and the rate of climb to 15,000 feet fell off only .4 second. The 1300 mile range was only 50 miles less than that of the A.

The B-25B was destined to take part in perhaps the most famous single raid of the war. The mission---the Doolittle raid to bomb the Japanese homeland! When this raid was in its early planning stages the B-18 was the first aircraft to be considered, though later this was broadened to include the B-23, B-25, and B-26. The B-18 lacked the necessary range, the B-23 was ruled out because its wing span was too wide to enable it to clear the "island" of our carriers. The B-26 proved to need too long a take off, thus clearing the decks, so to speak, for the B-25 to make history.

Lt. Col. James H. Doolittle, who was to lead the raid, selected and trained a group of volunteers taken mostly from the 17th Bomb Group and the 89th Recon Squadron. While training was going on the aircraft were modified to increase range. The ventral turret was removed to make way for a fuel cell which raised the fuel capacity to 1,141 gallons while subtracting 600 pounds from the empty weight. The maximum weight was raised to 31,000 pounds on take off but would decrease as fuel was burned enroute to the target. Other modifications included removing the secret Norden bombsight and replacing it with the 20 cent wonder, the Mark Twain, which was more accurate for low level bombing than the expensive and top secret Norden. Twin fake .50s of wood were installed in the tail to discourage stern attacks by the enemy fighters.

The USS Hornet, with 16 B-25Bs lashed to its deck, set course from San Francisco on 2 April 1942. The 18 April launch was earlier than anticipated but was rendered necessary when the task force was spotted by Japanese patrol ships. The Doolittle force bombed various targets including Tokyo and while the damage was slight the psychological effect was tremendous. Although all the B-25s were eventually lost, most of the air crews survived, and the overall effect seems to have justified the cost. As a morale booster to the American people it was outstandingly effective and the initial shock to Japan soon was replaced by a desire that it never happen again. Against that possibility four first-line fighter groups were kept in the home islands even though they were needed badly in the South Pacific.

In April other B-25s serving with the 13th and 19th Squadrons of the 3rd Bomb Group in Australia also were equipped with auxiliary fuel tanks, and along with a trio of B-17s, ten of them took off for a secret base in the Philippines. Arriving there safely they began operations from concealed airstrips deep in the jungle. In a harassment type of operation, they worked over Japanese shipping and supply areas, doing a lot of damage while avoiding serious losses. The rest of the 3rd Bomb Group was in action during this period against the enemy in New Guinea. From this point on B-25 participation in the South Pacific was on the increase.

The RAF received 23 B-25Bs as the Mitchell I with serials running from FK 161 through FK 183. These aircraft were not sent into combat, serving in training roles and for crew familiarization purposes.

Doolittle fitted two wooden rods into the plexiglas tailcone of his B to simulate .50s and hopefully discourage stern attacks. Other pilots quickly picked up on the idea, which soon became common. This pilot has even gone so far as to paint on false gun travel slots.

Tail Positons

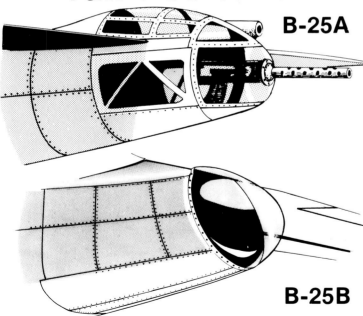

B-25A

B-25B

B-25B Number 13 of 17 Bomb Group in war games markings, May 1942. While most war games markings consisted of a White cross on a Dark Green circle, this one is obviously an exception to the rule. [D.W. Lucabaugh]

This B-25B at Wright Field in April 1942 was in the flight testing program. With the addition of the two turrets, the fixed .50 tail stinger was deleted along with the tail gunner's position. [USAF via D.W. Lucabaugh]

B-25 C/D

On 28 September 1940 the Army ordered an updated version of the B-25 featuring a number of modifications dictated by combat experience. This was the first of the series to really go into mass production. North American started manufacturing the C model on a line at Inglewood while the D Model went into production at Kansas City. The two models were actually identical in all respects and the dash model numbers and letters simply indicated which plant produced the aircraft. Deliveries began in January 1942.

An autopilot had been fitted in the planes flown by the Doolittle Raiders and this was now added as standard equipment on both the C and D. The Wright R-2600-9 engines were replaced by the more powerful R-2600-13 with Holly carburetors. A de-icer system, 24 volt electrical system, and larger wing tanks plus a removable bomb bay tank were fitted. This raised the maximum fuel capacity to 1,225 gallons for ferrying purposes. The bomb bay was enlarged and external fittings to carry bombs under the wings and a short torpedo under the belly were included. The .30 caliber nose machine gun was replaced by a .50 caliber gun and another fixed .50 caliber to be fired by the pilot was added to the nose. The turrets were retained though the ventral one was deleted on some of the early batches. An astrodome was included as a blister on the upper forward fuselage to enable the navigator to take star or sun fixes more easily. All changes usually mean added weight and the C and D models were no exception to this rule. Combat gross weight stood at 33,500 pounds on both. Despite the extra 100 horse power, top speed slipped to 282 miles per hour. The maximum take-off weight of 41,800 pounds was seldom used. Bomb load of 3,000 pounds was standard and 21,000 rounds of .50 ammunition was carried for the six guns. Under certain conditions the bomb load could be increased to 5,200 pounds by use of the external racks. The introduction of individual exhaust stacks for each cylinder requiring special exit fairings on the engine cowling gave later Cs and Ds an easily distinguishable identification feature.

Block numbers on the B-25C ran from the C-1 through the C-5, -10, -15, -20, to the -25. The D series ran through the identical dash numbers plus the -30 and -35. In all, 1619 B-25Cs, and 2290 B-25Ds were produced during the production run.

The RAF received the B-25C and B-25D models as the Mitchell II, getting 167 Cs and 371 Ds with serials running FL164 to FL218; FL671 to FL709; FR362 to FR384; FR393 to FR397; FR900 to FR939; FR-141 to FR-207; FV940 to FW280; and HD302 to GD345 plus KL133 to KL161. The Netherlands ordered 162 B-25C-5s to be serialled N5-122 through N5-283. Four B-25Cs were sold to the RCAF while 29 were obtained by the Brazilian Air Force under Lend-Lease.

Two B-25Cs were modified to become the XB-25E and the XB-25F, these were the first Mitchells to be given an X designation. The XB-25E was equipped with hot air de-icers for the wings and tail surfaces while the XB-25F received thermo de-icers in the same locations. These projects were eventually dropped, possibly because the Mitchells were being used almost exclusively in tropical or semi-tropical areas.

One B-25D was converted to be used for photoreconnaissance training as the F-10. As this proved to be relatively successful a total of ten of this version was acquired. The F-10 was given the more powerful R-2600-29 engines and were stripped of as much excessive weight as possible to improve both speed and range. Cameras were mounted in a tri-metrogen arrangement in a chin fairing. Other cameras were mounted in the rear of the fuselage.

B25C-1s of 310 Bomb Group fly low over the Mediterranean near Berteaux, Morocco to hit an Axis target. The C in the background, carrying its call letter Q, on its nose, is painted in the standard early war scheme, Olive Drab over Natural Grey. Note how the fabric covering of the rudders makes the OD seem several shades lighter. [USAF]

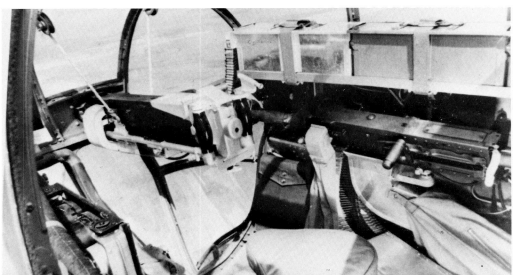

[Above & Right] Two cockpit shots show the instrument panel and left side controls. B-25 cockpits varied very little in the series. [N.L. Avery]

This interior shot of the bombardier's compartment shows the mounting of the flexible & fixed .50s and the associated ammo belts, shell & link bags, and bombardier's tractor seat. [N.L. Avery]

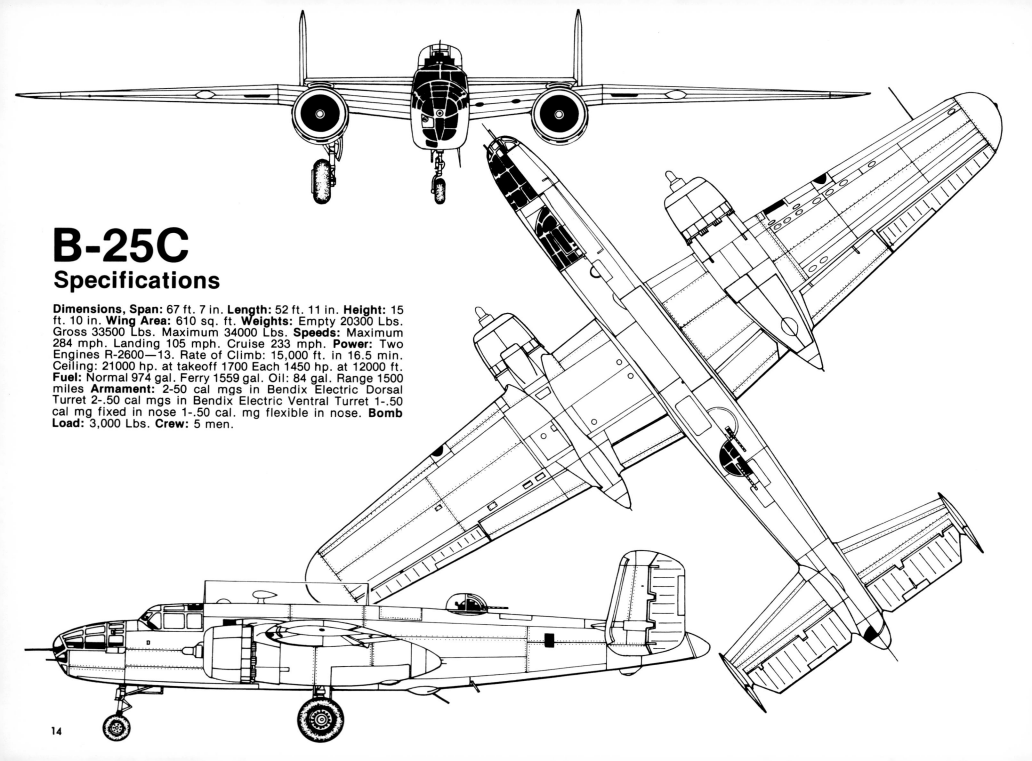

B-25C
Specifications

Dimensions, Span: 67 ft. 7 in. **Length:** 52 ft. 11 in. **Height:** 15 ft. 10 in. **Wing Area:** 610 sq. ft. **Weights:** Empty 20300 Lbs. Gross 33500 Lbs. Maximum 34000 Lbs. **Speeds:** Maximum 284 mph. Landing 105 mph. Cruise 233 mph. **Power:** Two Engines R-2600—13. Rate of Climb: 15,000 ft. in 16.5 min. Ceiling: 21000 hp. at takeoff 1700 Each 1450 hp. at 12000 ft. **Fuel:** Normal 974 gal. Ferry 1559 gal. Oil: 84 gal. Range 1500 miles **Armament:** 2-50 cal mgs in Bendix Electric Dorsal Turret 2-.50 cal mgs in Bendix Electric Ventral Turret 1-.50 cal mg fixed in nose 1-.50 cal. mg flexible in nose. **Bomb Load:** 3,000 Lbs. **Crew:** 5 men.

This shot shows a B-25C-1-NA of a training unit with a short aerial torpedo underslung for the anti-shipping role. [L. Hendrix]

Nose Variations

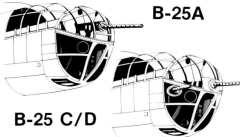

B-25A

B-25 C/D

"Desert Vagabond Jr," a B-25C-1-NA, of 12 Bomb Group's 434 Bomb Squadron over Tunisia in 1943. The name was prophetic as this Group operated in North Africa, Italy & the CBI and was in three different Air Forces. Only a very few of early USAAF aircraft to operate in North Africa carried the "British-Style" national tail flash seen here. [USAF]

Mitchells of 82 Squadron of 12 BG operate with RAF Martins over the Western Desert. Note P-40 escort just above turret of No. 33. The B-25s are camouflaged in Desert Pink over Neutral Grey. [USAF]

This Desert Pink B-25C-10-NA of 487 BS, 340 BG seen over Cap Bon, Tunisia. The patchwork to cover battle damage and over all beat-up condition indicates old 7A did her bit. [Robert Eby via Garry Fry]

A B-25C-5 in North Africa seen at Cap Bon, Tunisia. "Patricia Ann" made an emergency landing at 325 Fighter Group's base.

This B-25C-15-NA [42-32411] was photographed in August 1946 at Kiangwan Field, Shanghai, China. By this time, camouflage had disappeared, natural metal being the standard finish. As with most Mitchells, all armament was removed at the end of hostilities, the turrets being faired over. [D.W. Lucabaugh]

[Top Left] This B-25C of 83 BS, 12 BG is seen over North Africa, 1942. Note the escorting P-40 in the background.

[Left] This White tailed B-25 of 319 BG is seen flying over a snow-capped volcano. The Group flew B-25s for a short time only, late in the war.

Ventral Turret

Dorsal Turret

"Red Wrath" a B-25C-20 of the 345 BG's 498 BS Falcons. The White fin was the squadron marking for the 498th. This is one of the Cs or Ds "field fitted" with four .50s. The Plexiglas nose panels have simply been painted over.

"The Wolf Pack" of the 500 BS Rough Raiders, also of the 345 BG features similar nose marking with a horn added for emphasis.

"The Exterminator", a B-25D-25 [42-87450] shows the White tail marking of 499 Bomb Squadron of 345 Bomb Group. This Group, known for its gunship modifications, added fire power also to its glass-nosed aircraft. A second fixed .50 has been added to the nose and a downward pointing fixed .50 has been added to the tail.

A pair of B-25D-20-NCs of 42 Bomb Group, 13th Air Force caught by a cameraman on 11 April 1944. The 42nd was based at Sterling Island in the Solomons during this period. The figure on the nose seems to be a Mermaid which ties in with the name "Whirmaid." [D.W. Lucabaugh]

"Dirty Gertie from Bizerte," A B-25D-1, somewhere over North Africa, exhibits the wear and tear typical of aircraft in that theater. [F. Dickey]

"Pacific Prowler", also named "Jeanne - Queen of the Blue Grass", a B-25D [41-29710] unit unknown, appears to be returning from a mission.

A B-25D-5-NC of 490 BS, 341 BG in Burma, 1944, carries the squadron insignia on nose, which was a skull over USAAF pilot wings on a blue circle.

Cowl Variations

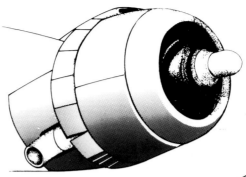

Early Cowling

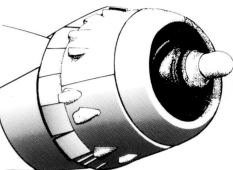

Later Cowling

A B-25D-10 [41-30278] of the 345 BG "Air Apaches", 500 BS "Wild Mustangs" is seen banking away from a burning target area. The white fuselage band was the 500 BS's identification marking.

B-25s of 42 Bomb Group on Stirling Island in the Solomons, warm up for take off to Hollandia Strip in New Guinea, 1944. [USAF]

This excellent pair of shots show the front and rear of "Pert' nint Poop", a natural metal F-10 ex-B-25-D-NC [43-3433]. Taken at Hickham Field, Hawaii on 19 March 1946, these photos show the nose mounted cameras and the field-modified tail position. [D.W. Lucabaugh]

B-25G

The type of targets in the Southwest Pacific Area were not suited to the massed bomber assault that was being employed successfully in the European Theater. While in the SWPA the targets were not as heavily defended by flak, they were widely dispersed and well camouflaged and thus did not readily lend themselves to high level precision bombing. New tactics were evolving that suited the conditions in the theater. Skip bombing, parafrag bombs, and strafing had been experimented with and developed to the point that gave maximum effect in jungle and island hopping warfare. Twin engine mediums were ideally suited to these conditions as they had the range, speed, and maneuverability necessary to the hit and run tactics and were more economical on fuel than their four engined big brothers. The B-25 seemed to have been designed with all this in mind. Above all, it was easy to adapt to the strafer role.

Lt. Col. Paul Gunn and Jack Fox, a North American Tech Rep had been modifying B-25Cs to this role in the Southwest Pacific with great success. They had started by adding a pair of .50s to the two already in the nose and eliminating the bombardier's compartment. Then they took out the ventral turret which had been a total fiasco, gunners were constantly getting air sick, the optical areas were usually coated with mud on take off, or streaked by oil in flight. Twin pods were placed on each side of the fuselage under the cockpit and fitted with .50s to give "Pappy" Gunn's B-25s eight forward firing .50 caliber machine guns fired by the pilot. They even added a pair of .30s in the landing bay light compartment in each wing. Last but not least in a few of the conversions, a 20mm cannon was fitted in the bombardier's crawlway. Later, after North American engineers protested, the .30s were removed from the wings. Flight testing had proved that these installations were effective after the skinning in the vicinity of the twin packs was beefed up and added bracing eliminated the cracking that had appeared along the wings leading edges between the fuselage and the engine nacelles. Ninety-seven additional fittings were fabricated by the people in the 4th Air Depot in Townsville.

All of this activity in the field led to the B-25G. After the successful mounting of the 20mm in the B-25C, experiments with the B-18A Bolo, the old Douglas that had been considered for the Doolittle raid, fitted with a standard Army 75mm Field Gun indicated that the B-25 could also handle the big cannon. Gunn's jury rigging had indicated that a cannon could be mounted in the crawlway and that it was the ideally location for the 75mm. The M-4 cannon measured 9 feet 6 inches and weighed close to 900 pounds. It was mounted in a cradle to absorb the shock and extended under the pilot's seat to allow for a 21 inch recoil. The navigator became the cannoneer. It was not an enviable job as slamming one of the 3 inch 15 pound shells into the breech in the limited space available required dexterity and strength. 21 rounds were carried. The nose itself was shortened and faired around the muzzle of the cannon. While "Pappy" Gunn had cut the crew of his modified Cs to three, the B-25G was intended to have a crew of four. The overall length was shortened to 51 feet. Maximum speed dropped to 278 mph. Twin .50s were mounted in the nose with 400 rounds per gun to enable the pilot to supress flak and serve as an aiming reference for firing the big gun. When the pilot had the tracers in line with his target he snapped off a round with the 75. The aircraft shuddered, some say it stood still, while others claimed it flew backwards for a micro-second. Later Gs had a tail gunner's position re-instated, mounting a single .50. Some also had the side blister gun positions also standard on later B-25s.

Under combat conditions the gun was found to be accurate enough but due to the hand feed, the rate of fire was low. Seldom could more than four rounds be fired during an attack. Further no evasive action could be taken when the cannon was used, putting it into disfavor with the crews. In combat the 75s were used against a variety of targets. Shipping was an especially good target as a direct hit with the cannon could sink most of the coastal vessels used by the Japanese. Even destroyers were sitting ducks for a flight of the B-25 cannon ships. The B-25 soon emerged as Kingpin of the Pacific because its chief competition, the B-26 was being sent to Europe. During the production life of the B-25G a total of 405 were produced at Inglewood. Two were sent to the RAF for evaluation but none were ordered by the British. As targets worthy of a 75mm shell got scarce, the gun was frequently removed and replaced by twin .50s.

Nose Variations

This manufacturer's photograph shows upper surface detail clearly on this B-25G-10 [42-65128]. Note the extra armor applied next to the pilot's position. [F.C. Dickey]

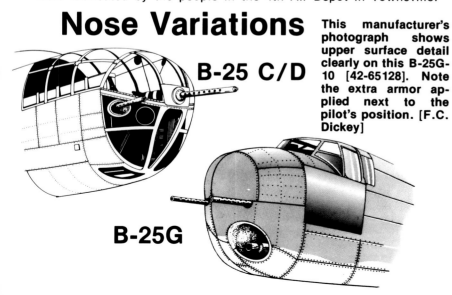

B-25 C/D

B-25G

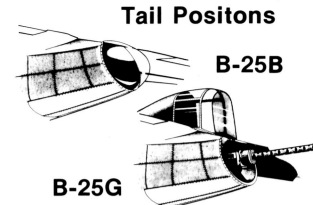

Tail Positons

B-25B

B-25G

A B-25G, "Blondie's Vengeance", is seen here in two photos. [Left] The plane is seen getting an engine check. Several pairs of G.I. shorts and socks flap in the breeze on a line strung off the tail. [F.C. Dickey] [Below] A sideview shows the blister and tail positions found on late Gs. This position, manned once again by a tail gunner, took over the now deleted ventral turret's role of protecting the plane from attack from below and astern. [USAF]

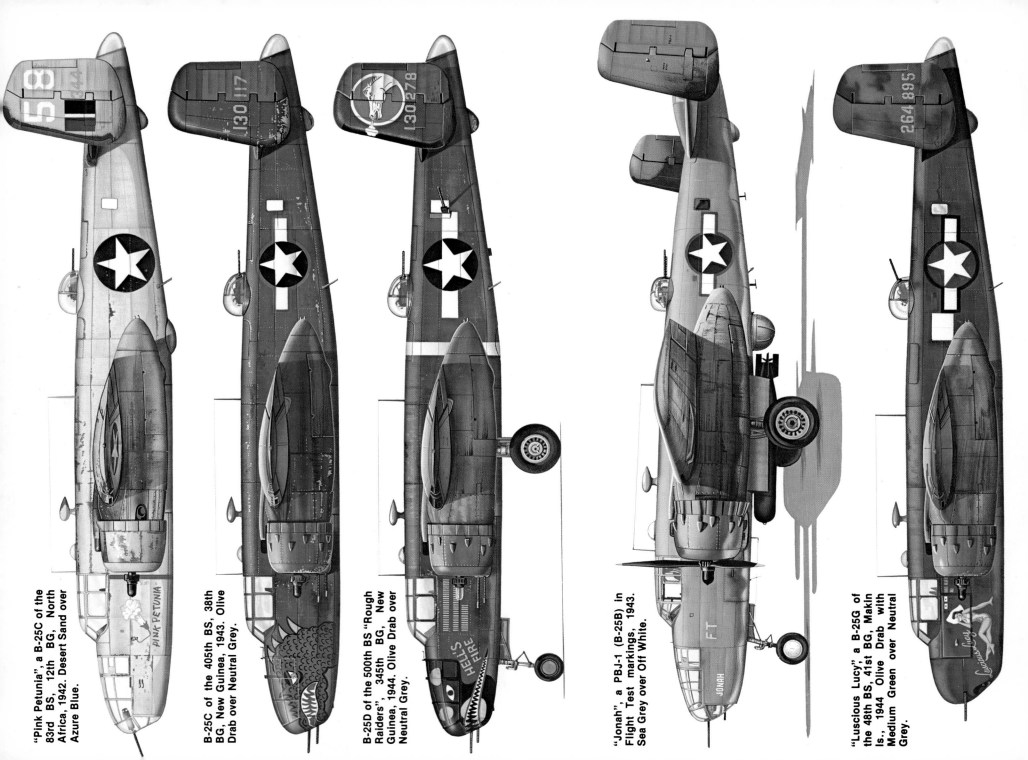

"Pink Petunia", a B-25C of the 83rd BS, 12th BG, North Africa, 1942. Desert Sand over Azure Blue.

B-25C of the 405th BS, 38th BG, New Guinea, 1943. Olive Drab over Neutral Grey.

B-25D of the 500th BS "Rough Raiders", 345th BG, New Guinea, 1944. Olive Drab over Neutral Grey.

"Jonah", a PBJ-1 (B-25B) In Flight Test markings, 1943. Sea Grey over Off White.

"Lusclous Lucy", a B-25G of the 48th BS, 41st BG, Makin Is., 1944 Olive Drab with Medium Green over Neutral Grey.

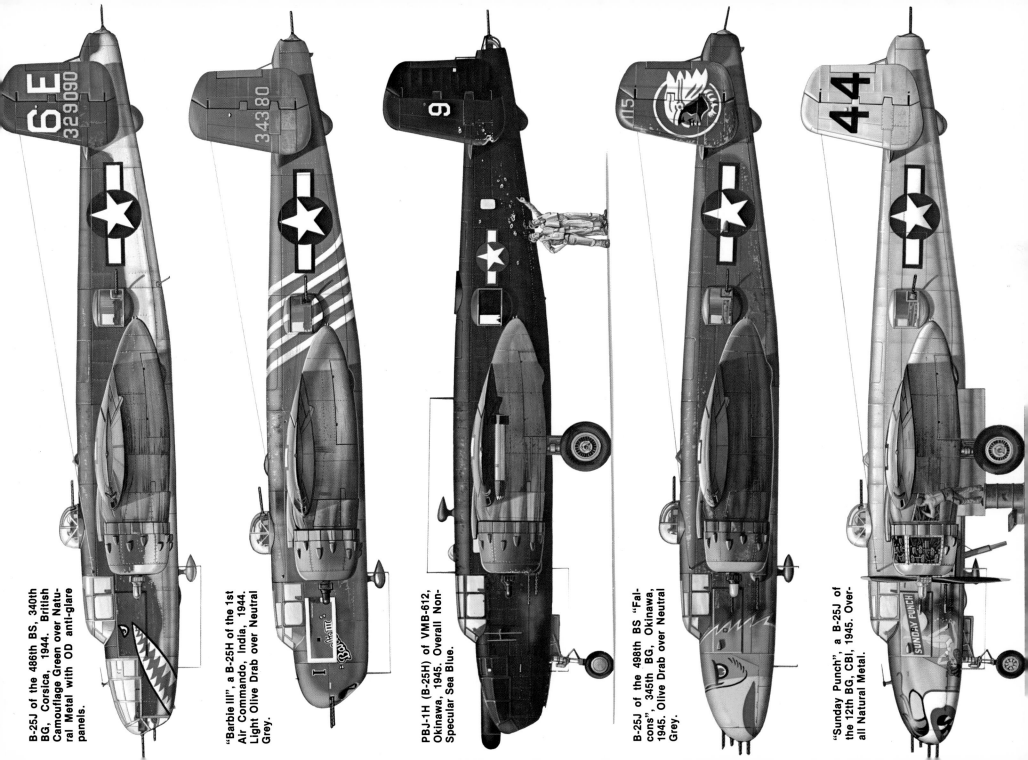

B-25J of the 486th BS, 340th BG, Corsica, 1944. British Camouflage Green over Natural Metal with OD anti-glare panels.

"Barbie III", a B-25H of the 1st Air Commando, India, 1944. Light Olive Drab over Neutral Grey.

PBJ-1H (B-25H) of VMB-612, Okinawa, 1945. Overall Non-Specular Sea Blue.

B-25J of the 498th BS "Falcons", 345th BG, Okinawa, 1945. Olive Drab over Neutral Grey.

"Sunday Punch", a B-25J of the 12th BG, CBI, 1945. Overall Natural Metal.

A B-25G of 38 BG's 823 Bomb Squadron shows that squadron's Tiger Head markings. As seen on 345 BG's field modified craft, gunships were often decorated with colorful nose art. The practice of using colored cowl rings as squadron identifiers was also common. [F.C. Dickey]

Side Blister

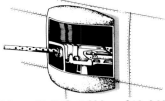

This B-25G-5-NA [42-64895] suffered a nose gear failure at Naval Air Base Majuro. "Luscious Lucy" bit the dust on 14 April 1944. This Mitchell was from 48 Bomb Squadron of the 7th Air Force's 41 Bomb Group. At that time, the squadron was based on Makin Island. [D.W. Lucabaugh]

The Black Panthers of 501 Bomb Squadron, 345 BG used this type of marking as a squadron identification. Several other styles were also used.

Armorers clean the 75 mm cannon of "Pride of the Yankees", a B-25G. Note the spent shell casings slipped over the .50 machine guns to keep dust out while on the ground. [F.C. Dickey]

B-25H

In August 1943 a more potent Mitchell, the B-25H, replaced the B-25G on the line at Inglewood. This version added a fifth man to the aircrew which now consisted of multi-MOS (Military Occupational Skill) people, only the pilot and tail-gunner having a single role. The others were Navigator-Radioman-Cannoneer, Dorsal Gunner-Flight Engineer, and Camera Operator-Gunner. As one wag put it, this enabled fewer people to foul up more areas than ever before. The top turret was moved forward to a point just aft of the pilots' position. The lower turret was finally completely omitted since it never had been successful. The tail area was redesigned to accomodate a gunner who operated a pair of .50 caliber Brownings in a mount similar to that on late Gs, with 600 rounds per gun. Barbettes or blisters were now standard on both sides of the rear fuselage and carried a single .50 machine gun each with 200 rounds per gun. The nose, however, was the position that received the most attention. The 75mm cannon was retained but was replaced by a new lighter type, the T13E1. Two more .50s were mounted in the solid nose and the two twin packs were retained and factory produced to carry 400 rounds per gun. Thus total armament was now one 75mm cannon, and 14 Browning .50 caliber machine guns. In addition the H could carry 3,200 pounds of bombs or a 2,000 pound aerial torpedo plus eight 5 inch rockets under the wings. The H model could be fitted with either the R-2600-13 or R-2600-29 engines, but as each produced 1,700 horse power at take off this made no difference as far as performance was concerned. A total of 1,000 B-25Hs were rolled out before production was discontinued.

The B-25H entered combat in the SWPA Theatre in February 1944. The same problems with the cannon as experienced with the B-25G plagued the B-25H and eventually most of these cannons were removed in favor of machine guns. There was no "I" model in the series.

Tail Positons

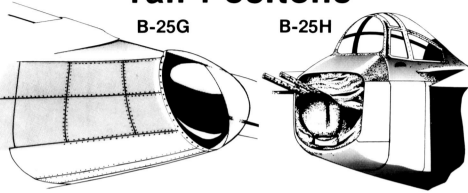

B-25G   B-25H

"Sweet Sue," a B-25H is seen here with two other Hs on the runway at Hailakandi, India, preparing for takeoff. These aircraft, painted in overall OD, display the five diagonal white stripes of 1 Air Commando. [USAF]

Nose Variations

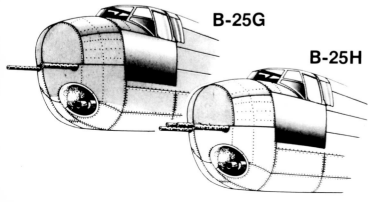

B-25G

B-25H

This B-25H-1 is seen at North American's Inglewood, California plant in a natural metal finish. This shot shows the add-on gun packs under the cockpit in great detail, as well as the four .50s that graced the nose. [Lin Hendrix]

This B-25H-5 [43-4448] has been mounted with a K-24 12 inch forward shooting camera in the nose, August 1944. [F.C. Dickey]

B-25H

Specifications

Dimensions, Span: 67 ft. 7 in. **Length:** 51 ft. 0 in. **Height:** 15 ft. 9 in. **Wings Area:** 610 sq. ft. **Weights:** Empty 19975 Lbs. Gross 33500 Lbs. Maximum 36047 Lbs. **Speeds:** Maximum 275 mph. Landing 105 mph. Cruise 230 mph. **Power:** Two Engines R-2600—13. Rate of Climb: 15000 ft. in 19 min. Ceiling: 23800, hp. at takeoff 17000 Each hp. 1450 at 12000 ft. **Fuel:** Normal 434/974 gal. Ferry 1624 gal. Oil 84 gal. Range 1350 miles normal. **Armament:** 75 mm nose cannon with 21 rounds. 2-.50 in top turret 4-.50s in nose 4-.50s in side packages forward firing. 1-.50 in waist on each side 2-.50s in tail stinger. 8-5'' rockets under wings. **Bomb Load:** 3000 Lbs. **Crew:** 5 men.

Three shots of 12 Bomb Group B-25Hs. [Above] "Old Bones," a B-25H-10-NA, the last B-25 off the line at Inglewood. "Old Bones" was signed by the war workers at the plant and sent to the war zone with the signatures and graffiti intact. It was assigned to 81 Squadron of 12 Bomb Group. [Left] This Group soon became famous for its colorful and frequently sexy nose art. "Swamp Angel" shows this to advantage. It shows also the tendency of 12 BG artists to use dogs to complement their cheesecake. [Below] "Vikin's Vicious Virgin" displays a more polished version of nose decoration accented with a nude wearing a Viking helmet.

B-25J [Mitchell III]

In December 1943 B-25D production was terminated in Kansas City in favor of the B-25J model which was to become the last production model. The 4,318 produced during its production run made the J model the most numerous of the Mitchell series. In addition another 72 of the Js, while not fully finished, were flyable and were included in the termination inventory when the line was shut down. As some of these were to see service after the war, it can be said that 4,390 J models had been manufactured.

The B-25J returned to the conventional bombardier nose with one or two fixed and one flexible nose gun. Four other fixed and six more flexible guns were featured in the same arrangement as the B-25H model. The crew was raised to six as the bombardier was returned to man the sight. Eight hundred of the B-25Js were built with a solid nose with eight nose guns upping the total of .50s carried to 18. This easily made the J gunship the most lethel twin engine medium bomber in the war.

The RAF received 314 of the B-25Js as the Mitchell III. RAF serials ran from HD346 through HD400; KJ561 through KJ800 and KP308 through KP328. Most of the Mitchell IIIs were assigned to the Second Tactical Air Force of the RAF.

Many of the bombardier nose Js were converted to the solid nose in the field using nose kits supplied by North America. Underwing racks were added on many to hold four 5" rockets. Another field modification was the fitting of a 150 gallon fuel tank in the radio compartment to add range.

This B-25J-5-NC [43-27793] flys West from Kansas City sporting a clean natural metal finish. The J was the first model since the D to sport the glazed nose. Note also that the B-25J, as with the H, had a twin .50 tail turret. [USAF]

One of the early B-25J-1s turned out at the Kansas City plant is seen here in flight.

This B-25J-10 shows the eight-gun nose arrangement which along with four side packs and top turret could bring 14 guns to bear on the target during a strafing run. Note that the inner side of both engine nacelles has been painted anti-glare Green.

This B-25J-5 of 489 Bomb Squadron, 340 Bomb Group, "Lady Elaine," shows the squadron code very clearly on a dark, possibly Blue, fin and rudder. Note also the similarly colored cowl ring.

B-25J

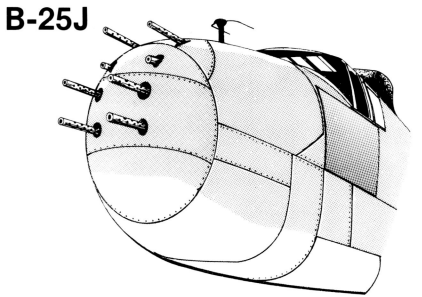

This excellent shot shows an armorer cleaning the eight .50s in the nose of this J of 500 BS, 345 BG. The guns are in position but the ammo chutes have been removed to allow better access. This photo was taken 25 June 1945 at Clark Field, Philippines. [USAF]

A bare metal finished B-25J-20 of 499 BS, show the "Bats Outa' Hell" insignia in Pale Blue.

A dash 25 [44-30852], undergoing an engine check. This again is a postwar photo. Note the faired over top turret position. [Lin Hendrix]

[Left] A rare photo of a U. S. Coast Guard Mitchell. This B-25J-30 was stripped of armament and used as a trainer/transport. [D.W. Lucabaugh]

This B-25J of 501BS, 345BG shows the Panther Head insignia to good advantage. The head is Black on an overall Red nose. While gaudy, this nose art is less flambouyant than earlier 345th examples.

22 BG's "Hotsee" is seen in this rare shot. Very few photos of this group are available. Note the unusual two-gun side pack low on the plane's side. This J has had a second fixed .50 added to the nose, a not uncommon modification.

This excellent shot shows the fin and rudder of 44-29775, a B-25J-20 of the 42 Bomb Group's 390 Bomb Squadron "Crusaders". The squadron insignia has been painted on quite large. Note also the rather fancy style with which the serial number has been painted.

"Alice-L" of 486 Bomb Squadron, 340 Bomb Group was returned to the States after piling up 40 missions. [Balogh via Menard]

These fine shots illustrate nose art seen on B-25Js of 12 Bomb Group. This Group's habit of mixing dogs and cheesecake is evident. "Milk Run", "Tail Breeze", and "Prop Wash" are comic illustrations of aviation terms. "Tail Breeze" was obviously a veteran, wearing a 100 mission indicator.

Two shots of B-25Js of 477 Bomb Group, an all-Black unit. This Group drew together four new Bomb Squadrons and 99 Fighter Squadron which had flown P-40s over North Africa. The Group was commanded by Col. Benjamin O. Davis, who went on to become the Air Force's highest ranking Black. The photo to the left shows a plane of 616 BS, that above of 618 BS. [Dr. R. Rose]

This B-25J of the 499 BS "Air Apaches", of the famous 345 BG displays a curious armament arrangement. Rather than use the available factory-kit, 8-gun nose, the armorers of the 499th have jury rigged a five gun set up adapted from a standard bombadier nose. As was the case with the early C and D gunship conversions, the glazing has simply been painted over. [USAF]

(Above) This B-25J of 498 BS, 345 BG, piloted by Major Jack C. McClure, Jr., Group C.O. lands carrying a Japanese surrender party, under the eyes of many happy GIs.

(Right) Another B-25J is seen at Nanking. Aircraft No. 316 sports a dragon and sun insignia on nose with Chinese national markings and serial number B31371. All armament has been removed indicating that this craft probably was used as a trainer. (D.W. Lucabaugh)

This camouflaged Chinese Nationalist B-25J was photographed at Nanking on 22 August 1945. The turret has been removed, but the plane retains the rest of its armament. [D.W. Lucabaugh]

Gun Packs

Single

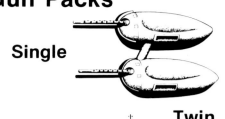

Twin

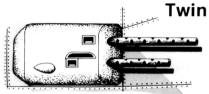

This Mitchell III of the RCAF is seen sporting an unusual marking scheme. This high visibility scheme probably indicates that this is a trainer. [D.W. Lucabaugh]

This B-25J [Mitchell III] of the RAAF is seen over Brisbane, late in the war. [Malcomb Long]

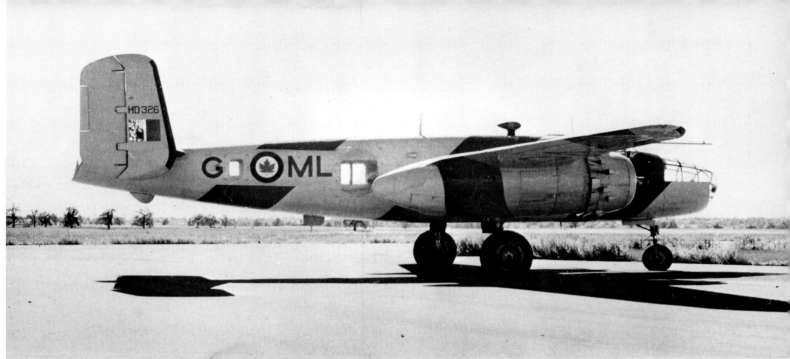

Three shots of Mitchells IIIs of No. 2 Squadron RAAF on the line at Hughes, Northern Territory in 1945. They appear to be in Foliage Green and Sky Grey camouflage.

The Mitchell in U.S. Naval Service: PBJ

The U.S. Navy received a total of 706 B-25s to be used by the U.S. Marine Corps aviation branch as land based bombers. The B-25B became the PBJ-1 while the B-25C and B-25D became the PBJ-1C and PBJ-1D respectively. These were used on anti-submarine patrol duties. The Naval version was equipped with radar and carried depth charges as their normal offensive weapon in place of bombs. They could also double as torpedo-bombers should the need arise. In this role they were the PBJ-1G. The B-25H was the PBJ-1H in the USN/USMC inventory while the B-25J became the PBJ-1J. The H remained about the same in Marine service as did the J except for some minor differences in the radio and other small equipment.

There doesn't seem to have been any special reason for the U.S. Marines getting Mitchells except that the Army Air Force had a surplus and the Marines apparently were willing to try their luck with the type. The thinking probably was that they could prove useful in close support of beachheads and landings.

VMB 413, the first PBJ-1 squadron, was commissioned at Cherry Point, North Carolina on March 1943. At that time the only Marine flight personnel were single place pilots, so VMB 413 in effect became a training squadron for navigators, radiomen, and gunners. These aircrews that trained with VMB 413 then served as the nucleus for follow on squadrons. On 15 September 1943 VMB 423, 433, and 443 were commissioned followed by VMB 611, 612, 613, and 614 on 1 October 1943 to complete the initial Marine Medium Bombardment Group. The first to be ordered overseas was the original squadron, VMB-413, which left for California on 3 December 1943 and thence to Espiritu Santo. In January 1944 the squadron began combat indoctrination training before going into combat from Stirling Island in mid-March 1944.

Initially operations were confined to night raids on Rabaul, Kavieng, and Bougainville. Soon daylight missons were started and flown on every third day. Despite heavy losses early in their career (two planes with full crews on 22 March, a ditching that killed two men and totaled the aircraft on 1 April, another plane and full crew on 21 April and a fifth PBJ hit by flak over Rabaul and lost with its crew on 5 May) VMB 413 received a Commendation from ComAirSols for developing bombing techniques and perfecting night intruder tactics. VMB 423 replaced 413 on Stirling Island on 15 May 1944 but 413 along with 423, 433, and 443 remained in the Solomons-Bismarck area until August 1945 when they were transferred to Malabang in the Philippines.

A total of nine PBJ Squadrons got overseas before the war ended. These Squadrons lost 26 Mitchells in combat and an additional 19 due to operational accidents while in the combat zone.

This PBJ-1B was phototgraphed on 31 May 1945. Of note is the single two gun pack on the fuselage side. The FT indicates a flight test aircraft. Note also the radome in the belly turret position. [USN via D.W. Lucabaugh]

This PBJ-1H [35277], piloted by Lt. Cdr. H.S. Bottomley, catches a wire on the USS ShangriLa, then taxies forward, completing the first landing of this type on a carrier. This took place on 15 November 1944. Note the Navy three tone camouflage. [USN via D.W. Lucabaugh]

[Left] "Jonah", a PBJ-1 with torpedo and ventral radome, is seen undergoing flight testing in this shot. The aircraft is painted in faded Intermediate Blue with a Grey underbelly.

[Above & Below] Two Marine Corps PBJ-1Bs are seen in flight near Turtle Bay, Espiritu Santo, February 1944. [USN via D.W. Lucabaugh]

This shot gives a clear view of late war wing-tip radome, which replaced the earlier ventral mount. The undersurfaces of later PBJs were the lighter Dove Grey.

This PBJ-1H, seen on the ramp at North American's Inglewood plant, shows the tail hook position to good effect. [D.W. Lucabaugh]

This PBJ-1J [64976] has the radome on the wing tip and a full complement of add-on guns. [USN via D.W. Lucabaugh]

Miscellaneous Mitchells

War Weary B-25s were turned over to the various training commands to be used as flying classrooms and for other training purposes. The B-25C, D, G, and J became the AT24C, A, B, and D in that order and later they were redesignated as TB-25C, A, B, and D respectively. A number of these Mitchells were assigned to Yuma Army Air Field in Arizona late in the war and used in the BTO school there. Many WWII vets will recall that the popular definition of BTO was "Big Time Operator" but in this case the initials stood for Bombing Through Overcast. The school was set up to train bombardiers in the new techniques of radar bombing which would enable them to locate, and hit their targets even if it was totally obscured by cloud cover or darkness. Many training flights were made from Yuma to the coastal cities of Southern California. The aircraft would fly out over the Pacific Ocean and then turn in towards the coast and the bombardiers would pick up their targets electronically and make dry runs on the such cities as San Diego or Los Angeles. The program was supposed to develop trained men to locate targets in Japan or Europe should the war continue longer than expected. Other B-25s were converted to high speed transports after having all turrets and guns removed.

The B-25 series served with a number of Allied nations during the war and on into the postwar era. A complete roll call of nations operating the Mitchells with totals where known in parenthesis includes Australia (147), Brazil (29), Canada (100+), Nationalist China (131), Peoples Republic of China, France, Great Britain (561), Republic of Indonesia, The Netherlands (249), Peru, Russia (870), and Venezuela.

In the post war period the B-25s like other obsolescent aircraft were turned over to the National Guard units. Others were turned over to MATS, SAC, TAC and ADC. Some went to individual air fields to be used as hacks, and some released as war surplus found their way into civilian use. These in many cases underwent transformations that turned them into rather plush company aircraft or private airplanes for wealthy individuals. A few went to collectors and to museums for display purposes. Still others were pressed into civil use as firebombers and crop dusters.

This B-25D-35-NC, "My Buddy," has been fitted with the BTO [Bombing Through Overcast] radar array under the nose. It is seen over the Pacific approaching the California coast on a training mission. [F. Dickey]

After the war, most B-25s that were kept on inventory were disarmed. Most were used for training duties, as with this spectacular, Red-marked example.

This B-25 has been assigned to MATS [Military Air Transport Service]. [F.C. Dickey]

This B-25J was photographed at Andrews AFB in 1947. This aircraft was one of 72 that was not completed or accepted contractually. It was flyable and turned over to the Air Force as part of the termination inventory. The belly radome is very similar to the AN/APQ-13 housing carried by B-29s. [Bernie Ederr via D.W. Lucabaugh]

Most Air National Guard units flew the B-25 at one time or another. B-25s or TB-25s of four ANGs are seen: Pennsylvania, Michigan, Oregon, and Massachussetts. The war-time BTO bombing radar has now been replaced by a more sophisticated version in the nose radome. [Balogh-Menard]

U.S.A.A.F. Bombers
of the Second World War
in Action From

1144

1063

1134

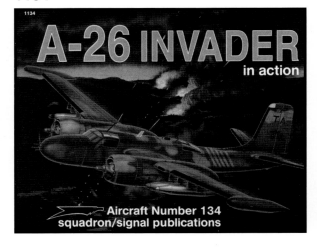

squadron/signal publications